The Light Between

The Light Between

POEMS BY

TERRY BLACKHAWK

Wayne State University Press
Detroit

16 15 14 13 12   5 4 3 2 1

Library of Congress Cataloging-in-Publication Data

Blackhawk, Terry, 1945–
The light between : poems / by Terry Blackhawk.
p. cm. — (Made in Michigan writers series)
ISBN 978-0-8143-3614-4 (pbk. : alk. paper) — ISBN 978-0-8143-3615-1 (ebook)
I. Title.
PS3552.L34235L54 2012
811'.54—dc23
2011035241

Designed and typeset by Maya Rhodes

Composed in Charlotte Sans and Scala

For Neil

Contents

Split the Lark—and you'll find the Music—

Emily Dickinson (J 861)

i

A Peaceable Kingdom

—after Ed Fraga's *La Santa E Gloriosa Carne*

This dream is too dry:
it takes moistness to survive
the night, not broken towers,
flattened obelisks, hills
reclining like a sluggish lover
beneath a sun-bitten sky.
So this is how it feels
when the wind comes
scratching at that door
you closed: your pillows lie
abandoned, an erratic landscape
chisels into the marrow
of your sleep. They've got
a sale on plots like these,
and they've saved one
just for you. Let this emptiness
be your permanent bed.
No king spread these sheets.
No queen will stretch
from satiny sleep bearing her peace
like a cup of blessed wine
into the day. Oh shadowy
swiveling angel, is it enough
to let light fall
on half a face?
If a door exists in every story,
a window in every dream,
this vacant bed

might still conjure flesh,
conjugality, mirrors that glint
with what could have been: a blue frame
extending out, a checkered
pathway in.

Medea—Garland of Fire

i.

Jason, I despise this aging
dowager you make of me, a sexless
queen, her womb gone dry and the teeth
of love gnashing nothing but air.
These days I think emptiness
enrages most, flesh that cannot forget
its hunger turned to anger, blown
useless petals. Among my people
women have ways of remaining
supple with desire. Why do you scoff
at these offerings?

Rampant, how I desired you
as I stood in my father's palace, stared at you
and burned. The glare from your sword
dazed me, set my mind
babbling with visions, I was that full
of leaves, breath, movement between
my legs a mouth an eye
beginning to leak.

ii.

Since only innocence can protect a warrior,
I unearthed from the fragrant ground
the tenderest bulbs of spring and from them drew forth
a clear, resilient milk. It turned you
pliant beneath my hands as I massaged it
onto you, half drunk and nearly wild
with your scent, your skin. Laurel
and sage, yes, but I was cunning, to shield you,
oiling, kneading you, all the while
taking care to think—think of the enemy,
my father's dragon, how to help you
escape his flames.

I gave poppies to the dragon—poppies from fields
where once I wandered, my mind filled
with constellations and art. I saw patterns
everywhere and everywhere plants
revealed their inmost dew.
I cannot recall learning my medicinals,
these teas, tisanes and infusions,
but there was nothing that would not release
its secrets to me. All mine. My art.
My growth. This flourishing. This is what
you have taken from me. I have no language
to replace what I have lost.

iii.

The children I would bear from this
burning—could they but crawl back
through the gates of my womb
to climb in reverse my tree
of life. I would have them come to me
solemnly, bearing their golden curls
back, back, up and through
branches, twigs and leaves
until they dissolve into the darkness
I gave them.

I long for fields, the nodding assent
of flowers. Surely you—wilderness-raised
on Chiron's slopes—also chafe against
these sophistries. Or have you stayed too long
in the princess's bed? A political match, you say,
but I think you tasted more than power
at her bosom. Vile alliance. You who never knew
a mother's milk or passion of original touch—
it was I who awakened you to the ways of women.

iv.

How eager I was to let you become
plow to my willing soil, to succumb
and give you back the sweet and trembling
dark. Only later, dissembling
for my father would I deny the way
you came to me as I lay
beyond reckoning, glowing and gold
as your hair in the torch-thrown flames.

                               How cold
you could be, you and your blue-eyed kind,
I'd come to learn as your frost ruled my mind.

Yes, I have refused to worship
your clear-eyed deities, logicians
of city and state. Refused to hear the reason
in your tones. Me? Reasonable?
Reasonable to attire myself in gray
and walk these corridors
a vapid shadow, reviled for every
hair on my head, mockery
of a queen, effective as dust.

v.

If I have turned from the green earth,
if I shall never see my footprint pressed again
on dewy ground, never breathe
the mist my garden breathes or pluck
the finest blooms to weave, crush, enmesh
in my hair or drape across this
aging bosom—one blossom at least is left me.

Here, amidst walls and pavings, slaves and stones
whisper against me and the mourning dove
patronizes with its coos. Patron?
I have only you in this place where all I hear
are palace doors clanging—or corners, nothing
but corners—this labyrinth you've wound me in.
But I have sworn no Greek will scorn me.
I shall form a garland of revenge.

vi.

Have you ever looked into a fire, seen
its embers glowing and desired it, whole?
Gold, Jason, gold. Haven't you yearned
to run your fingers through the molten
nuggets, to become embedded in the burning
and enamel yourself, Midas-like? The glint
in your eyes reveals the alchemy you long for.

Soon, you'll see . . . soon, soon. I wander
from this last encounter obsessed with how best
to betray you. My fingers twist my hair into knots.
My tongue licks without warning from the corners
of my mouth. I'll design a gift of pain disguised.
My blaze dies down to coals, but hers shall rise.

Cunning, curled, the ivy's lines
I'll turn bright gold—seductive vines
to brand into her brow a flame
erasing father, kingdom, name.

vii.

At least this sometime pleasure—
that at whatever hearth my heart
shall cease, I shall have had some time
to watch its embers soften
on the stones, while she, pale wench,
will sputter mothlike, casting about
in the fiery net I set for her,
untangled, sparkling, beautiful—
until she puts it on.

viii.

I feel so dizzy standing here, a silhouette
propped against these columns. This trick of lighting
from behind my back turns me to shadow
and from across your proscenium I appear
two-dimensional, a figure made of dark. I know
you plan to cast me, bare-headed, down the white
stone road, but you do not understand the role I play.
The moment I step away, the whole scene will tumble down.

ix.

The small reversals I expected—my graying
edges, a more balanced, settled need for you. Not this
major blight of fortune, outcast from city,
heart, hearth and all.

                         Oh Jason, the grove
we could have tended is gone. Orchard island,
exiled notion—it drifts farther and farther away
from our shore, smoldering trunks hacked apart,
blackened branches as faggots piled. I see its thin smoke
riding through the ocean air.

                            I will put on a shawl
                            of smoke and haze. Drape myself
                            in the gray peace of the dove.
                            I will be, quietly, like ashes
                            concealing fire.

Out of the Labyrinth

Rotten Cotton, Little Yellow Jacket, Slingblade—
when they burst from their chutes, a cowboy gets
eight seconds to ride, else lose to the sawdust floor.

I have seen a bull toss then try to gore its rider
before trotting away elegantly, delicately,
as if sniffing some distant air—as if sensing

smoke or whiffs of lies—the way yours
hung in the air between us those last days
you sat in your chair not speaking—glowering
at the animals lunging on the screen.

Replay bathes the beast in a golden, slowed down
light—an aura, a cloud, a mythic trick I do not
fall for. No garlands adorn these massive heads

and fringed cowgirl groupies make no ritual
in their name. The whirlwind has no name,
you said of your tribe's dust devils that bore

dead souls across the plains. 8 seconds, more or less,
30 years, more or less, and I'm back in our dissolved
and dappled past—still apt to cringe, weep at the mute
mail you forward, terse notes of interest to be paid.

Little Yellow Jacket, Rotten Cotton, Slingblade—
When does wreckage begin? Your mother threw
your jar of marbles, your childhood's shining prize,

down the outhouse in an outburst of rage.
Mine said she wished I'd never been born.
We had no wedding photo, just a print

of a red-faced sculpture that amused us,
a cowry-bedecked tribal couple stuck
in a dime store frame. I wore a borrowed dress
before the judge that flouting, devil-may-care day.

Loose a bull from its pen, it corkscrews out into
the arena, snorts, contorts, tosses its shit-smeared rump
up into the air. We never spoke of the night

you came home drunk, with a swollen, blackened eye.
I was pregnant by then but I heard you cry "Terry,
Terry, do you love me?" Had you staggered in,

tried others' doors? The car you would retrieve later
was left blocks away. Afraid to face you, silly,
I thought, of course I do, I sighed, never sensing
how much you needed, how much I denied.

Is this what the ancients tried: to master tons
of mean monster muscle, to worship the bull
from the sea, the power of surges and tides,

to contain its snorts and rolling eyes behind
a slatted grate until—(Say grind, rage, leather
strap; say no, your words were not a wall of fury)

it explodes—(Say no, I did not fling coins
in anger; say no, you did not sneer at me

or lie)—until it explodes outward with a tight-
jawed, bare-handed human clinging to its side.

Rotten Cotton, Slingblade, Blueberry Hill—
they storm out of the labyrinth of fences into
the whirlwind of shame. In the end that unbridled

drama was all we shared. I cheered Wiley Peterson—
Shoshone like you—hero of hanging on. I kept
a false face in the face of your pride and tried

like a clown to divert you, all the while clinging—
clinging still—as if to the brindled back
of Blueberry Hill—a love song I wanted to ride, hold,
however I could, to whatever would connect us.

Belated Figures

i.
Cicadas pulse the night—
Today, an emptied hull,
Its claws clasping the lip
Of the frame beside my door.

Wrens that burbled all July
Have headed south.

I walk these rooms
As if I could find the edges of my
Life. Not a memory that doesn't
Hold you in it. To name them all
Would take another thirty years.

ii.
How could I have failed
To grasp your hostility? Silences
I accepted without question
As if the act of love alone made you
True.

iii.
The thinnest limbs hang without moving . . .

. . . motionless, the way
You lay beside me, refusing
To move or turn, a sarcophagal carving,
                Frozen

With anger.

iv.
It was winter by then.
A few weeks later
I would climb out of your car and feel you
Watching me, a red-hooded figure,
Disappearing
Through the snow.

From the Roof

Shingles, asphalt sheeting, strips of lath—
                       it was a torrent, a deluge
of old boards sliding down, a rushing
            rain of splinters, crumbled shakes and thatch

while overhead the Mexican workers
                whistled, sang and seemed to tease one another,
their laughter a counterpoint to the rhythm
                    of hammers and nails. I heard the pulley

hauling up loads of new shingles, a clanking
                funicular scaling the roof as steep
as the one my neighbor's daughter
             had to be coaxed down from after her boyfriend

carved her name in his chest,
              which makes its own counterpoint to the sure-
footed cheer of those Mexicans, or were they
         Ecuadorans, their ease of angles

and altitude learned alongside tooth-like
              mountains that seem to scrape the sky.
My son had teenage rooftop moments, too,
           as when, reckless with intent, he climbed

and steeled himself against
             the chimney, propped there with his camera
making the acute angle work
            for him, one leg stretched almost beyond

balancing, craning for the right shot
    while the raccoon mother and her babies
made their scrabble down the shedding
     bark, scratching off swatches

of messy maple. He'd yearned to catch
     the furry bundles emerging
from that trunk, a good two-thirds of it
      hollowed by rot for years.

Years, too, since the creatures
     disappeared from that tree,
even before I moved away from its
    central mother trunk, sheltering limbs.

The roof went up just as the world
     fell down around it,
the marriage a cascade of breakage, the way it
      gathered momentum, accelerating,

filling my dreams with broken windows, charred
      frames, the nursery on fire, another woman
laughing in the next room, poison ivy
    coming up through the floor.

And who'd have thought a slow rot
      would have such fervor to it, such sheer
ferocity when it came to the cleaving
    of our bond. Think firestorm,

shock wave—that deluge. It raged, it rained,
    it lashed the limbs we had tied against

the storm, uprooted the hedges, denuded

our Rose of Sharon.

Shall I find cause in the bird feeder

he shinnied up the trunk to mount,

after a while left dangling, empty, my part

of the bargain—I admit. I admit.

I broke it. I failed to feed. Or is it better written off

to something less specific, some universal

dark matter, the source I'm told of an

unexplained gravity, a force so fierce

even birds take flight, though I recall a time that tree

held ten different species, all at once,

on the same day, and I'm only half surprised

to call it now a gather of delight.

Ginkgo Autumn

In Asia, male and female Ginkgos are planted in
pairs to ensure a fruit whose white, satiny seed is
harvested for medicinal purposes.

November brings Ginkgo sheen and squish—
a shining carpet
of rained-down yellow leaves dotted

with fallen fruit I tiptoe to avoid.
The glow beckons: step inside despite
the stench.

***

Some harvest the foul-smelling
fruit, roast or grind its seeds as potions
taken to balance yin and yang in
the body.

         In Hiroshima, four
"silver apricots"—the only survivors
of the blast—sacred stand.
Our city cuts female Ginkgos down.

***

Ginkgo, honored dinosaur tree,
against its reptilian bark I see

the scarred hide of that alligator
we watched in the Everglades, rising

from the swamp in thrashing contest with
a python—the gator's grinning jaws

pinning the neck of the snake, thick rolls
of snake coiling the gator's body.

We shared a keen astonishment
then—before his bitterness set in.

***

Scarred tree, sacred tree—
prehistoric mystery, tonight's
security beacon turns its branches
to strobe-lit cut-outs of dangling fluted
fans.
	They hang without stirring,
not clattering or tossing like the palms in Key West,
nor struggling against themselves
like the two-headed fish
I saw once, going nowhere fast.

***

And as for the years he tossed
like fish, back into the water? Caught,
then discarded, I'm told a fish
will continue to swim without its head.

***

Turning our mattress
after several years

I found only one body's
indentation: mine.

***

There would be no coaxing him
back to our bed, but this has nothing to do

with the Ginkgo, there was nothing I
could do or change.

***

Oh woman, the frail tissue of your sex
suggests a lonely drift of leaves
amongst whose limbs once came pecking

his "one-eyed vireo"—gleeful coinage,
sweet delight, the full thrust of bird
in hand or—dare one say it?—bush.

***

Ginkgo, fossil tree, ageless herbal
remedy—from below us thermal
forces rise. Tell me, how does it happen—

the leaves beginning to fall this way—
a few more brilliant days and then, as if
on schedule, their golden letting go.

***

Look closely at the leaf of this tree.
Note the dispersing pattern: the veins
fanning out from the center, dividing

in twos. I misspoke before. This has
everything to do with the Ginkgo.

The Burn

I saw it once in a sycamore
at a fishing spot near the lagoon,
one of the tree's three trunks combusting

from within—flames inexplicably
licking out into the otherwise
cool and moisture-laden autumn air.

Perhaps a cigarette or careless
spark set it ablaze, though the pulsing
seemed to swell from its core. An inner

rot may have ripened it for burning.
They say fire in the wood's a fiction,
but I know what I saw. Like some scars,

I cherished that burn. I did not try
to put it out but kept circling back—
months, years—to investigate the char.

Wild Bird Rescue in Key West

What if there had been no rising wind
the day we booked the snorkel trip
out to the reefs past Key West?

What if the tour had embarked, taking us
far enough over a smooth ocean
to dive and find ourselves, astonished

and new to each other, as glistening
and colorful as fish? What if we had
made of it an underwater playground?

Instead, we took in the pelicans,
your *bill holds more than his belly can*
burdening the poor birds, as they splashed

in the wildlife rescue shelter, batting
one another with long bony beaks, a batch
of large Browns, like toddlers in a tub.

On a nearby pickup, a Palm Warbler
with yellow under-butt and bobbing tail
preened in the side-view mirror

as if flirting with the bird it found there.
Were we ever adequate as mirrors
to each other? Aside from the limerick,

which annoyed me, you do not appear
in my scribblings of palm fronds, banty roosters,
or bougainvillea barely responding

to the breeze. If the eye chooses what
the heart suspects, today I read storm warnings
in retrospect. For us, there would be no rescue,

no stories to retell. Just a Green-backed Heron
missing half its upper beak or the baby
Broadwing hopping on its one good leg.

I've kept that small Haitian painting, the one
you didn't want me to buy. In its foreground,
a wedge of Great Egrets soars

above an azure bay. The artist paints them
as if from a cliff, looking down a great distance
at their delicate, fleeting flight.

Chambered Nautilus, with Tinnitus and Linden

Is it crickets, a thin wind across a wire,
hiss of spindrift off the crest of a wave,
or radio emissions from a planetary probe?
When I took the hearing test, this sound
I carry nearly drowned out the faint high or low-
pitched pulses of air I strained in order to "pass"
the test to hear—each tone becoming ever more
soft, so barely there I could almost see
it disappear—just as I've often strained
after birds in the farthest reaches
of the canopy. Call it a squint of sound,
tone on the edge of not existing at all
a hint, a sleight of breath—a flutter on the branch,
bare after-image of the spot from which
desire just—took wing.
                            Dr. Seidman calls it
a phantom phenomenon—lost hearing
reminding the hearer of itself—lost sounds
trying to make themselves heard. I make them ghost
sounds, haunting neural tin-pan alleys where syn-
aptic nitty gritty saints go marching intra-
cellular-ly. Call it mitochondrial fizz,
call it not-so-good vibrations—bits of DNA
decoding, or decaying, along the dendrites tip-
tapping the cochlea. It is static, uni-
                            linear, all pervasive in-
vasive, this persistent insistence. I will color it
empty flat sizzle not to be tuned
out—or away. But ah, to listen differently—

to pick up and put back down again
the shell against the ear, to feel the reach
and return of one's pulse traveling
through a golden mean. Shells do that, I mean—
arrange themselves in proportional beauty. Take
the Nautilus whose chambers catch and toss
back the rhythm of the wave—all heart and shush
echoing yes   listen   really   it *does*   sound
like crickets. So let us think again, of crickets,
yes again—and luminous evenings—and the beauty
of *again* again. How modest and mere those
myriad insects those summer nights our son
                    had just turned three.
There was music and a pulse to the background then.
And did it come from two hearts humming
                              or the echo from
that tree we loved—the heart-shaped leaves
of the heart-shaped linden, with its pour
of pollen—a buzzing fragrance of blossoms
and in every one of them a bee.

iii

Walloon Lake, Opposite Shore

The tiers of blue-green hills
that stretch from the other side

of this lake then plummet
to Lake Michigan's shore—

I have divorced them. Just as I
divorced the haze that rose

from the dune we ran,
shrieking, down—then climbed

back up, his legs
ascending ahead of mine.

And I have divorced
the roads we traveled and the waving

fields that found me heavy
with yearning, and yearning—

yes, I have divorced that, too.
Now I am wed to these willows,

their fronds add a soft
mutter to the breeze. And as for

the couple who chat nearby
in Adirondack chairs—

What I want to talk to you about,
later, he says. She laughs,

flashes a scar, keeps the banter
going—for them I have a proposal.

They can keep the banter and the laughter.
I'll waltz off with the scar.

The Lost Life List

Surely not the worst of my losses,
the places, species, dates—*Point Pelee, 5/7/93*—
Blue-gray Gnatcatcher—Carolina Wren,
all tucked inside a guidebook that is gone.

But when my friend asked which rare sighting
I "grieved most to lose" in order to put
my loss in her poem, I thought how grief
magnifies the smallest things—lips tight shut,
a single leaf in unsuspecting light—
and did not choose to share.

After I took her call, I went for a walk
by the river.   It was a late October morning,
bathed in golden fog. The willows
were in perfect dying blaze, synchronous
with mist so thick it seemed to brew the light.

Who could see, let alone lose a bird
in such dense air? How be anything but lost
in that shimmering cloud?
                         From overhead,
beside the bayou at the far end of the island,
came a heavy, almost maritime crank:

the sound of the wings of swans in flight.
Their mechanical downbeats, so close above
but cloaked in fog—I neither saw nor lost them.
Nor did I lose the voices of men singing

as they fished in a foreign language—
and the boomboxes from picnic grounds
on the other side of the trees
seemed filled with intent to be found.

Litany of loss and leaves, tailor made
for mulling. It was all trumpet and bass,
all poem and shine. It was endless,
forgiving, and I had already lost it,
even though it was mine.

For the Mothers at Sundown

Your embroideries have outlasted the vats that dyed the threads:
So many threads, there is no way to isolate a single one of them.
Earth colors, derived from clay, sumac or hickory, seep or rustle
In your work. Your interwoven greens dream secret crevices:
Hills that dipped to shelter under outstretched boughs where you'd hide
As winds whipped by, then stake the everlasting flags of childhood
Claiming each bower as yours. Your clairvoyant blues suggest
Small lakes and streams concealing creatures you'd strain
Water through your fingers for. Sparkling surfaces, they gave back
The light of your days and taught you, when you fished, to let hooks
Do minimal harm. In pasture corners overgrown with brambles
And brush you collected berries, made trails, felt out the traces
Of those who went before. Yes, you stitched the yellow alphabet,
Proverbs, the schoolhouse, its bell. You struggled with floral chains
And knots, balancing hoops that stretched fabric taut,
Palms pricked by the red injustices hidden underneath.
Now you know laughter's a song to keep fingers flying, invention
A guise for the edge of the frame. There you place embellishment:
Knobbed threads that add new twists—intricate vines, silken
Petals—to your chain of losses, patterns that say to us:
What better use of sorrow than make a blossom of it?

Belle Isle Solitary: New Year's Eve

Today, as I walked along the river
and it seemed possible to feel the year
holding its breath, a kayaker's paddles
suddenly sliced by. I wanted to give you
that sidelong surprise and also the jay
skulking in the scrub and then as well the hawk
boldly fanning its wing and tail. No leaves
obscured them. The current carried floats of ice,
a freighter lifted its wake and went on
through misty air, and the sky was a bell
waiting to be rung. I call it *mi vida,*
even this loneliness, even if I carry
only half of a song.

Along Blue Ridge Parkway

at the crest of a hill
a shirtless boy,
about eight years old,
runs barefoot with easy,
methodical intent, past
a stone wall and nodding
strands of phlox. I turn
my wheel and think
he could run like this
forever, the dust
a coating of pollen
on his glistening
sun-browned skin. Behind
a heavy summer haze, mountains
loom like intuition.
My partner is miles away,
his bed half empty,
like this road I'm driving,
through waves of heat,
heading down toward town.

Cosmic Enterprise

Sun going down. Warblers chipping
at their business. Mine's interpreting the air,
air upon skin, thinnest vibrations.

When troubled, look around: name five
new things. So Self Help counts bromeliads
bursting along a branch, and look—

the palmetto's become a pineapple,
or an armadillo, a prehistoric something
or other. Odd, how a setting sun

suggests a chill despite the sky it glorifies
with gold. *Every day is a journey*, wrote Basho,
and the journey itself is home. Here. Here.

Here. Here. Here! calls the cardinal. A catbird
mews raucously from the shade, breaking
the peace of one less day.

Standstill

Those summer sundowns
the drought
brought the gardeners out—
watchful waterers, participant
observers, who would
if they could reverse
the cloudless skies.

The whole season
was like that—
the savory dried
in its bed, our spindly
impatiens and long
exhalations.

Only our maple's
itinerant hive seemed settled
into usefulness.

One evening, rooted
with my rake, I watched
as bees rose above
the rooftop, soaring
pinpoints, fuzz in the sun.

I craned to catch in each
glowing spot
some disappearing
purpose, but got
no closure, idling neutral

bypassed by passing
minuscule errata
on airborne
errands, charging
particles—

now matter, now
wave.

The Hawk in Winter

The hawk in winter works these roadside trees,
sits plump and stolid as a hefty fist
until some furry bit it scents, or sees,
then spreads, fall, mounts again to thicken 'midst
the empty branches. Sometimes a squirrel's nest will
catch my glance and turn my motoring eyes.
It's not the feral bird, though just as still.
Yet winter drives may foster true surprise
as from far northern ranges drifted down
hawks guard assorted posts along our high-
ways' fume and flow. What wind is it that's blown
them here, to perch, to peer as we pass by?
Like feathered gargoyles from some distant age
wild wonders watch our daily pilgrimage.

Winter Solstice, Rosedale Park

I've cleared the walk of ice
and snow, and now another fall
reduces the world

to black, white, shades of gray.
Down the block, my neighbor's
an abstraction: shadow

body with arms and shovel
flinging snow through filmy air.

Time was, to mark this solstice
I'd step into the clear dark, cut
fresh holly, set a single candle
against a single pane.

Today, a slow no
stalls the season to a slow
now. No rush, flush of mind,
matter, no bright creatures

fleshing themselves out
onto fields of surprise, or praise.

Fog yesterday. Snow today.

Perhaps a third eye's on the pen
while a second mind retrieves
what the first mind's gone

to sleep on. I write *windy*,
mean *weedy*. Think *perch*,
write *purchase*. Each mis-

step makes more sense
than slippage. And the finches
I've tried to leave out

of this poem? They're the ones
seeking both purchase
and perch. They cling

to the maple's ragged bark,
grip the cable the feeder
swings from. Fierce, feathered

hearts, they will not
dissolve into the mute
distance. And Mind, dear fierce

feathered Mind—
what will you find to hold onto?

iv

Skywriting: Volusia County, Florida

The J and the E were already in place
By the time I saw their puffs adorn the air
Fathoms above me, there on the asphalt,
Where I stood gazing.

Make it *jetsam, jellybean, jewel* I thought,
But the script unfurled, straightened then curled
Into the beauteous swirl of an S—
Thrilling, unfolding.

It should have been easy to predict. Even
Summer sky's a canvas for Belief, here
With rooftops, posts and stumps all proclaiming
Jesus as Savior.

On then to the U's first side:
A furrow that grew at full throttle,
Plowing the sunlight, seeding the blue with
Harrowing cloud lines.

I wondered if the pilot was alone
And if, as he sat working the controls,
He saw his Faith writ large through derring-do,
Fearlessly flying.

Perhaps he was a ragged Soul pouring
Pious smog across an unsullied sky
In some last desperate act with which
No one could quarrel.

Or simply call it Enterprise, a contract
With a preacher, say—the larger the purse
The bigger the script—to lead his Faithful
On to the Rapture.

By now the letters had begun to wisp
Away. I did not stay to learn whether
Jesus ruled or saved. I left as the lines
Disappeared quickly

Toward Heaven—or not—while the difference
Between Need and Belief blurred like smoke feathers
Fading through air into the hope that
Something will save us.

Lot's Wife

—after the sculpture by Kiki Smith

Then salt erupted
through me, bursting like seedpods,
a hissing vapor.

Now I say my gaze
will be last to go. It is
the lifetime that's passed

I struggle to see,
not this road pocked with thermal
brine, an angel's hand

forcing me forward.
I strain to hear our vanished
fountain's music fall,

but I've no magic
to turn mirage to marriage
again. Here I stand,

an eroded wife,
utterly lacking in grace.
Drop by drop, grain by

relentless grain, salt
trickles down my corroded
breasts and thighs. The wind's

leathery lips skim
my skin. I have no names now—
sister, mother, friend

all sucked into this
high hot air. I've heard of tribes
to the south who lave

and bathe, oil and wrap
their beloveds' bones before
re-interring them

in the earth. Each year,
they enact this sweet respect.
Yet dare I call it

sweet? My bones crumble
and fade. Once I believed in
the sweetness of salt.

Now all I know is its burn,
its millions of tiny flames.

Diagnosis

The sutures tattoo our worst fears
into place. Yet the surgeon remains
optimistic. Time, it seems, is all
he has to explain, and plenty
of it, five good years, or fifteen.
So many hopeful treatments nowadays.

But in my dream I have the same
bad news as you, a shadow
across my shoulders. Here I am
in a blue striped shirt
on my knees beside a draped
shape, box or bird cage,
it's about half my height,
covered in black. Inside
is a uterus—yours, or mine?
Creature or blossom, I must
shield it from the policeman
who sniffs, points his nightstick
toward the screen, set like a small TV
into the cloth over the womb.
He turns a channel and the game
is on. A figure stands
in the batter's box, takes
a swing. A strike. Another swing.
This time the ball flies foul.
Strike two. The cop leans closer,
pokes a stethoscope toward
the cage, where beneath the cloth

I can feel our heart/organ beating, beating—
it's a small batter, battering against
the wires, it's pushing from inside
with wings, or scissory legs, frog or bird
I can't see what it is but it's all
I can do to protect it through the windup,
the swing, the attempt at flight.

Dear Luis

Sublime calls today—the entire canopy
Alive and singing—
As I gaze at my last card from you,
Dear Luis. Edward Hopper's *Seven AM* 1948.

Sixty years and the sun still rises
On the plain New England storefront.
I will not see it sixty more.

In memoriam, I will put you
In that tumult of greens left
Of the store. Perhaps a whole town
Stretches down the street to the right,

A procession of doors and windows,
Angles and squares, filled with lavender
Shadows, and all as uninhabited

As this corner beside a woods
That fills a frame. Beyond
The pharmacy, with its boxes of light,

Branches flow like waves.
I will find you in there, somewhere,
As birds begin their morning

Song, each day, all over again from the trees,
While in the bright-washed, unopened
Building, the shade in the southern

Window will remain half-drawn
And the clock on the northern wall
Will point to, and probably chime,

The time. Blue bottles in the window.
A few signs. The cash register waits as always
For business to begin. Not a soul

In sight, just scathing light as the sun
Makes its daily creep up the path.

Torque Dancer

Elaborate hand gesture: middle finger lowered
the other three erect and what can
the opposable thumb oppose? His whole
body's in opposition, but he's at one
with the air, moving, skewed slightly
along Woodward Avenue. An off-
kilter lilt to his frame, he drums
his different march along our street,
upper body torqued a quarter turn
from the vertical, head looks west,
arm waves east in regular intervals.

Hardly ignorable, he's ignoring
yet bonding us in apprehension
of his display. Say he does see us—
not as onlookers exchanging knowing
glances—but as minions, taking places
in this parade he is so clearly
the drum major of. Or is he conjuring
a swarm of angels? Perhaps they fill
the sidewalk from Central Methodist
to St. John's Episcopal with its banner
"Pray for the Tigers Here."

Now he squints and peers at the ball park
across the street, through a carefully held,
invisible lug nut, poised like a lorgnette,
its aperture framing images in some private
picture gallery. He's in there, somewhere.

Only a part of him is here, dividing us,
his audience, as he passes through us,
the momentarily motionless, where we stand
on the red carpet that's been duct-taped
to the sidewalk beneath the marquee
above the polished brass Fox Theater doors.

Christmas Eve at the Atomic Carwash

Usually I ride, but today I've walked the length of the carwash,
passing air fresheners, scrapers, decals, caddies for trash,
to sit on the vinyl bench and watch the revolution
of brushes. The windowed wall fills with steam as slow-motion
Medusas writhe in currents of synchronized spray. Outside
the day feels underdone, wreathed in fog and oddly mild.

Like underwater corals, the felt heads press forward and I guess
I'm no less smug than the next citizen. I pass the homeless
with their signs, and now these carwash workers: I wouldn't know
their names—just "Earthman," whose moniker stuck some summers ago
from neighbor kids keen to mock his ceaseless walks, bare chest,
matted beard and braids dangling down his leather vest.

What planets do we offer one another? What centers to lean on?
I nod and smile, thankful for my tankful, my sudsed-up car, gone
but not off track. And what's this coming to me now, digitized,
some tinny intonation that makes one guy say, in mock surprise,
"Aw, man, that ain't shit." I wince, too, at the discordance
and look behind me, less object than effect of his observance.

On the wall above, three red plastic bells, capped by a gluey
snow, blink and ring in seasonal harmony, pinging singularly
like a harpsichord in a stony room. The pings grow tinier,
tinnier, chiming *the holly and the ivy* and *all the flowers*
that are in the wood, but here it's the brushes' chrysanthemum
heads, lights flashing, the hot wax spitting its puny stream—

and Earthman, my attendant, snapping a towel from the huge glass eye
of the drying drum, and my little car emerging just at *Hark!* By
the Herald he's on it, white cloths flapping, this earth angel,
swabbing, polishing, brightening the shell
until I rise up, drop spare change in the tip box, glad for the shine,
and cross the rubber mat, its striated puddle, the thin and parallel lines.

A Visit to the Gallery

—at the Detroit Institute of Arts

Use your eyes, the guide sings out. *Children,*
this is the See-More Camp, we're going to move
quickly so use your eyes. Why is that lady
naked? pipes one brave boy
below her bellowed *Eve, by August Rowed-on.*
Clearly she's entranced herself. No nasal *anh*
has colonized her heartland, and Van Go's
no *Goch*, he's just the way we learned him,
lore passed on, just like his ear, which—
she chirpily assures—is real, everything here
is *the real thing*. Eve's anguished, twisted
form's mere nakedness but they're progressive
verbs, learning in one-stop-shopping
the grown-up game of name-it-and-go,
learning that to see more is less,
unlike poor Seymour Glass beside the waves,
overwhelmed by the more that poured over him;
or poor Cezanne who, despite the apples
and stones the children of the town rained down
on him, made pilgrimage after pilgrimage
to his outlook on Mont Saint Victoire.
Here's one of more than sixty canvases.
It doesn't show the aqueduct, houses,
the quarry placed like an abyss between
the viewer and the inaccessible
peak. No dust, pressure, or heat.
It's serenely blue, and I'm settled on my campstool
in front of it—this concert of blues

Rilke might have named: *a densely quilted blue*
among the closer trees, *a listening blue*
where light falls on the upper slopes;
the sky's *a self-contained blue, a bourgeois*
cotton blue, and when will these children
name their blues if all they use is their eyes?
No time to get lost looking, no chance to see
with the curious heart—they must follow
in her wake, their joyfully ducky guide,
a Julia Child of the galleries, leading her small
foot soldiers from Auguste to Vincent,
from sculpture to portrait to Paul *Go-gone.*

Writing Magritte on a Moebius

—after *L'homme au Chapeau Melon*

I am writing the raised
Armpit of a dove, feathers thick
As an unmowed meadow.

I am burrowing
into the articulated underside
of the wing. I am entering

the chin and the hat,
the bowler hat, behind the wing.

My students write a rain of
hatted men, a door admitting a cloud,
lips that fill a sky.

We are following an alphabet,
mediating a mystery, meditating

on a Moebius.
Our eyes scan Magritte
while the infinite

topological surface pulls
our minds past
the crumbled plaster

of this room where we sit
ten stories up
as the setting sun

turns city rooftops
inside out.
How simple the Moebius, the one

twist of the strip
of paper that turns two
dimensions into three.

I do not know which dimension
these feathers come from,
sucking out my breath

my cosmopolitan air
broken by wing beats, wing
beats, wing beats.

The strip slides beneath my pen.
My words will dissolve

in a plumy blur,
wrap back and loop themselves

again. A white vision drapes
my eyes. My shield is the blue

Heaven behind me, and is love
the dove that seeks to undo
my craftily knotted tie?

v

The Eggplant

Today, in my sweeping, my Swiffer pulled out,
From behind the kitchen cabinet, a desiccated
Eggplant, shrunken and flattened down.
With the sunken stem curled in its center,
It suggested a plum on a Japanese scroll,
But I knew it was an eggplant
And I gave praise to the eggplant for keeping
Its form, even as it shriveled to this light
Porous thing—a dried vegetal discus
That I could flick across the floor.

Obeying laws of collapse there in the dark,
It had released no swarm of fruit flies,
No scent of rot or mold, into my unwitting air.
Secret nightshade, sucking in its cheeks,
Drawing the luscious skin down, emptying
Cells in slow abandon—it had kept itself
For me to discover, to pick up and test
The exquisite husk. It had transformed
Silently, and without obvious flourish,
Until I poked around and found the beauty of it.

I think of my ex-husband standing in sunlight

but it's a frozen tree frog I hold
in my hand, capturing the evening
sun as it slants through the palmettos.

He's hollowed, stiffened in position,
and I balance him on my desk top
poised and posed like a football lineman

ready for the hike. One leg stretches
twice the length of the forward-crouching
body making a stem I can twirl

between my fingers. The other forms
a Z, its toenails barely touching
the desk, as if he's about to spring.

Decay would not have left him so fixed
and exact, like a paper lantern
or a cicada's husk. Some abrupt

and thoroughgoing freeze must have caught
him thus, midstride, his claws still clinging
to the bark. Hold him up to the sun,

the spine's an X-ray, the skull a dark
spoon above half-closed eyes, crescent slits
admitting light. The dried pod of him

fairly glows, revealing veins, vessels
still red but no longer pulsing. I
wonder what he saw as the cold fell,

if the lids lowered as the blood slowed,
the abdomen puffed out, innards turned
to vapor and he became his shell.

Possum Trot

And here comes Senor-Herr Possum, whiskers all abuzz,
belly scraping the ground. Nosing. "Unc' Billy"
covers the garden slowly, now here, now there where Mr. Fox
dallied with his Missus, both of them lolling in the snow
early last winter. Bright. Hot. Furred. *O give it up, luv,*
Fox seemed to say to her: *I am dizzied by the way you*
go on and on, putting each dandy delicate foot
half on the soggy chrysanthemums, half arrowing less
into my heart than casting a web around it. Dazzling paw spinner,
jouster d'amour, I am the beginning, middle and end of a queue
knotted only to you. How can we not knot together in this crisp,
luscious air? Their late foxy He/She—a whiff Possum now noses. *Cheerio*
mates, he says, *it's all grubs to me.* No fuss or fusion,
naught left to His Inspectorship but this quasi-conundrum:
odiferous histories that rise like spirits, creep and crawl
past and through the mulch he so ploddingly reads. Track
quester, transient four-footed savant, he makes his nightly hajj
right on time: 11:00 P.M., the petunias, 11:05 the patch of zucchini.
Sluggish snout pusher, midnight marsupial, is he heedless of the lush
terroir he savors, its lingering tremors, the hot shuddering
under fur and skin? Their winter yips climbed a treble clef of
viscera, their yowls plummeted down a bass clef whose
wild moist midnight scales Possum's nose has text-rayed,
X-rayed or taken in as a tonic. What to do with vanished music?
Yippee, he twitches. Fox trot, foxy love, hum it limb to limb.
Zany honey fox song, swing a song to tiptoe to: gone but for the aroma.

Marriage Poem

You are the children who came through us
into your lives. You are the courtship dance
of the whales you saw from the beach
at Santa Monica, your first Valentine's Day
together, two leviathan hearts surfacing
from the generosity of the sea.

You are the man who carried a ring
in his pocket as you walked with your woman
through the streets of San Francisco,
your secret joy so visible a homeless stranger
stopped you to say, "Son, you better
put a ring on that lady's finger!"

And you are that lady, the woman
who carries her lily like a torch,
spilling fragrance from the star at its center.

Now we lace our gratitude through your hands,
blessing the children you were and the children
you are ready to bear. You teach us how
we may inhabit any point in time, doubly
and equally, like that Easter morning we gazed
at the Pacific from a rocky slope, Marin County

and the continent stretching behind us.
Today I look back at my looking
and find in you the center of the circles
described by two great Redtails, the breathless
pivots of their swoops and dives, their soaring
connectedness, the light between them.

—Ned and Birgit, June 30, 2001

The Whisk and Whir of Wings

This is for the hummers
Who hover over the outstretched palm
Of the woman in Louisiana
And for her summer day, her cotton frock,
The makeup she did not use
As she sat stock-still in the moment
Of the birds, a mini flock of them,
Whirring in place above her.

And this is also for the drummers
Who know a beat can occur in the mind alone,
The body absorbing the idea
Of the beat—the least whisk of wire
Across a drum's taut surface:
Even if it does not touch—that gesture
Entices our nerve endings so we
Think we hear *swish, shush, brush.*

                                                    How soft
And suggestible we are, to let the mere notion
Of a thing tremble in us. How variable and virtual,
The paths of sound. The deaf percussionist
Knows this: her strokes feather,
Tam tam, wing beat, just above the frame.

Give her a glimpse, a riffle in the leaves,
And her brain creates "a corresponding sound."
She says we can feel a vibe, even before we see it—
Which must be why these creatures,
So lately landed in my in-box, have led me

To the hum, the drum, the dream.

                                  Still, love,

It is not the idea of these Ruby-throats
You sent compels me, rather their palpable
Jeweled bodies, poised above the woman's lap,
Stalled and seeking the nectar
She offers. I believe her palm holds
The rhythms of the birds, motionless,
Waiting, as she does, accepting the way
Their wings disturb her air.

Not Wafting, but Dofting

... floating around the corner it came,
the first scent of spring, the giving of new aroma,

or "dofting" as Swedes would have it:
dofta, to smell, emit fragrance from within.

Our "smell" oozes over into "stink,"
but these fresh daffodils, these apple petals

do not smell, they doft, saying *breathe, become*
the green again. Imbibe the air. Oh love,

I learn you through this unblemished word.
It's you I inhale this morning.

Let words go a'winding, planting their flags
on the wind. You're dofting, you tell me.

Of course, I say. Waft may carry the sweetness.
Doft unfolds the bouquet.

Imagining Billy

It is not hard to imagine Billy Collins
stretched out on the bed beside me
in the place now occupied by his new
and selected poems. He is wearing
striped pajamas, in a lightweight pale
blue flannel with a darker blue piping,
purposefully selected for their classic,
formal lines and the way the colors
enhance the lucidity of his eyes.

Unlike me, Billy has closed the book
he was reading before bed and placed it
on the nightstand alongside his water glass,
watch and ring, admiring surely
the peaceful arrangement of the objects
and the way light from the hall glances off
the watch and the ring and places a small square
shimmer on the glass—a Vermeer-like touch
he will save for future reference.

And unlike the volume of his poems,
which lies where I left it, face-down
and half-hidden in the covers, Billy
is a picture of composure—
hands clasped behind his head, his gaze
sailing quizzically around the room.
Perhaps he is interrogating
the snow or coaxing bands of mice
from the elegant labyrinth of his mind.

Perhaps he is devising a plan
to introduce the curtains
to the windowsill, the alarm clock
to the bedside lamp. It does not matter to him
that I lie here, ready to fool with
his buttons, or muss the remaining
hairs on his balding boyish head.
He has deeper mysteries to probe
than my unambiguous flesh beside him.

Into the Canopy

All day we have walked
the swamp and I wonder
if peace or the idea of peace
coats the water. Tonight
making love I close my eyes and see
the limbs of trees
as if I am a child looking up into branches
a child spinning around one point repeating
one word to the edge of its meaning
over over *marimba marimba*

White ibises float, wheel
descend dizzying from behind
our backs where the forest is darkest
they float and land, float and land
flocking into the canopy and when he
enters me I see them flapping and hear
my throat's birdlike cries

Glossy, taut, the water stirs with
hidden life, reflects
night, branches, stars, surface
tension, my jaw, straining
for release, I am moaning
rolling down into sky,
moss, stems, currents, the fragrance
that rises from the water, world
before peace, before name

Flowing into clear darkness
nothing coats it, this river miles wide
not peace, notion or name
but waters move within me
and when he stirs them
small lizards leap
from twig to leaf, stem
to branch and along the branches
plants attach themselves, bromeliads,
claiming the air around them
those bits of bark they cling to
where they send forth tongues of flame

Meditation in Green

Birds flutter, chip, vanish.
Their loss makes a current: swish, disappear.
Light on the high wire—beckoning silence.

It's not birds I miss, perpetual
workshop: their flittings distract me
from understanding green:

new timbres of green, multiplicities
of green: green fronds in a green
wind, whole childhoods

of green. In air this clear,
it is not enough to say: that arc
opens, these flight lines

close, nor to note
how what lies closest to the trunk
is the softest green:

the curliest, duskiest
green: mosses, lichens,
epiphytes that live on air.

Earth's water ignites
my green. Green fires
in the blade, sparks into

pine needle, palmetto spike,
mangrove, or fern. Green bursts to differ
lest it drown in an ocean of green.

Beyond the margin of trees,
clouds carry our names.
Light on the high wire—brightening silence.

Acknowledgments

Ambassador Poetry Project, http://ambassadorpoetry.yolasite.com: "Torque Dancer"

America: "The Hawk in Winter"

Borderlands: "Lot's Wife"

The Bridge: "Along Blue Ridge Parkway"

Comstock Review: "Imagining Billy"

Driftwood Review: "Standstill"; "Not Wafting, but Dofting"; "The Burn"

Dunes Review: "From the Roof"

Ekphrasis: "A Peaceable Kingdom"

English Journal: "A Visit to the Gallery"

The Florida Review: "Ginkgo Autumn"; "Wild Bird Rescue in Key West"

The MacGuffin: "Medea—Garland of Fire"; "Winter Solstice, Rosedale Park"; "Belle Isle Solitary: New Year's Eve"; "Marriage Poem"; "The Whisk and Whir of Wings"; "Possum Trot"; "The Eggplant"

Nimrod International Journal: "Out of the Labyrinth"; "Chambered Nautilus, with Tinnitus and Linden"; "The Lost Life List"; *"I think of my ex-husband standing in sunlight"*

Platte Valley River Review: "Meditation in Green"; "Into the Canopy"

Syracuse Writers Anthology: "Skywriting: Volusia County, Florida"

Third Wednesday: "Christmas Eve at the Atomic Carwash"; "Diagnosis"

U.S. 1 Worksheets: "For the Mothers at Sundown"; "Belated Figures"; "Cosmic Enterprise"

"The Eggplant" is online at http://pplpoetpodcast2008.wordpress .com/2008/04/29/terry-blackhawk/ *Princeton (NJ) Public Library Poetry Podcast*

"Medea—Garland of Fire" appears in the chapbook *Trio—Voices from the Myths* (Ridgeway Press, 1998).

The editors of *The MacGuffin* nominated "The Whisk and Whir of Wings" for a Pushcart Prize in Poetry.

"Out of the Labyrinth" was published in *Nimrod* as finalist for the 2009 Pablo Neruda Poetry Prize. "Chambered Nautilus, with Tinnitus and Linden," "The Lost Life List," and "I think of my ex-husband standing in sunlight" are in *Nimrod* as winners of the 2010 Pablo Neruda Poetry Prize.

Patricia Hooper, Judy Michaels, Desiree Cooper, and Mary Jo Firth Gillett and her poets of Springfed Arts are among the many friends and colleagues whose insights have helped inspire and refine these poems. Special thanks to Molly Peacock, Francine Ringold, Carol Was, Gregory Orr, Marie Ponsot, Alison Granucci, and the staff at the Atlantic Center for the Arts. I am grateful as well to the Detroit Institute of Arts for the invitation to lead workshops on writing about art where some of these poems began. I also extend great gratitude to Annie Martin and Wayne State University Press.

Notes

"Medea—Garland of Fire"
Medea's name derives from the same root as "medicine," indicating her
  identity as a healer as well as a sorceress.

"blue-eyed kind"—Medea was from Colchis on the Black Sea; hence a
  foreigner or other to the Greeks.

"Chiron's slopes"—According to legend, Jason was abandoned by his mother
  at birth and raised by centaurs.

"white stone road"—Jason was preparing to banish Medea and her children
  into exile, where traveling without protection would have amounted to a
  death sentence.

"Out of the Labyrinth"
I am indebted to Bill Harris for "mean monster muscle."

"From the Roof"
The phrase "some universal/dark matter, the source of an unexplained
  gravity" is borrowed from Matthew Olzmann.

"For the Mothers at Sundown"
This poem is dedicated to Miriam Polli Katzikis. "Let hooks do minimal harm"
  is from Marie Ponsot.

"Writing Magritte on a Moebius"
This poem stemmed from an exercise described by David Morice in *The
  Adventures of Dr. Alphabet: 104 Unusual Ways to Write Poetry in the
  Classroom and the Community* (Teachers and Writers Collaborative, 1995).

"The Whisk and Whir of Wings"
The phrase "creates a corresponding sound" is from "Hearing Essay" written
  by Scottish percussionist Dame Evelyn Glennie about her deafness. http://
  www.evelyn.co.uk.